# Positive Ninja

## ACTIVITY BOOK

Ninja Life Hacks™

# Welcome

Hi there, ninjas! My name is Positive Ninja. My book is packed with everything from fill-in fun to puzzles and games.

This book belongs to

........................................................

........................................................

Come and hang out with me and my friends!

## FEELING DISCOURAGED?

Just pick up this book and discover fun new ways to boost your mood! As well as puzzles, there are helpful mindfulness and breathing techniques for you to try out, too. And the best thing about them is that you can take these with you wherever you go—they can be your secret weapon to feeling positive!

# Contents

# All about me!

Grab your pens and pencils to fill in these pages with everything about YOU!

My name is ..................................................

I am .................................................. years old.

I live in ..................................................

I live with ..................................................

..................................................

..................................................

## Check the words that describe you:

- ☐ Confident
- ☐ Leader
- ☐ Shy
- ☐ Kind
- ☐ Friendly
- ☐ Loud
- ☐ Quiet

Draw or describe it here!

My favorite colors are . . .

This is my home.

Color them in!

Draw yourself in the space,
then color it in.

This is what
I look like.

Ninja Life Hacks™

# All about me!

## My best friends are . . .

.......................................................................

.......................................................................

.......................................................................

.......................................................................

## My friends would say that I'm . . .

- ☐ The leader
- ☐ Positive
- ☐ Loud
- ☐ A good listener
- ☐ Funny
- ☐ Kind
- ☐ Shy
- ☐ Sporty
- ☐ Artistic
- ☐ Adventurous

## What do you prefer?
### (YOU CAN ONLY CIRCLE ONE)

MORNING   or   NIGHT

TIME ON MY OWN
or
TIME WITH FRIENDS

ADVENTURE
or
CHILLING OUT

ART   or   SPORTS

VIDEO GAMES   or   TV

DRAWING   or   BAKING

PARK   or   THEATER

ICE CREAM   or   CAKE

SUMMER   or   WINTER

# Complete each sentence by circling your top choices.

1. I would choose a pet . . .

CAT   /   DOG   /   GUINEA PIG   /   FISH

2. I would choose to live . . .

AT THE BEACH   /   IN THE COUNTRY   /   IN A CITY

3. I would choose . . .

TV   /   BOOKS   /   VIDEO GAMES   /   MOVIES

4. I would choose to go . . .

BOWLING   /   SWIMMING   /   BIKING   /   HIKING

5. I would choose to play . . .

OUTDOORS   /   INDOORS

YOU ARE AWESOME! REMIND YOURSELF OF THAT FACT EVERY DAY!

# All about me!

## Check the things you like to do in your spare time!

- ☐ Reading
- ☐ Drawing
- ☐ Playing sports
- ☐ Swimming
- ☐ Watching TV
- ☐ Hanging out with friends

## My Favorites!

Movie: ..............................................................

TV show: ..........................................................

Book: ...............................................................

Day of the week: ...............................................

Animal: .............................................................

Snack: ..............................................................

Place: ...............................................................

# THINGS THAT MAKE ME SAD!

Check the ones that make you feel sad, then write some of your own.

- ☐ People that are mean
- ☐ Feeling tired
- ☐ Feeling hungry
- ☐ Being too busy
- ☐ ......................................
- ☐ ......................................
- ☐ ......................................
- ☐ ......................................
- ☐ ......................................

# HAPPY THINGS!

Check the ones that make you feel good, then write some of your own.

- ☐ Listening to music
- ☐ Dancing
- ☐ Vacations
- ☐ Being kind to people
- ☐ Helping people
- ☐ ......................................
- ☐ ......................................
- ☐ ......................................
- ☐ ......................................
- ☐ ......................................

# FEEL GOOD FUN!

Everyone feels sad or worried sometimes, but there are lots of things you can do to change up your mood.

Which ones will you try?

Get creative and make something!

Bake or cook with your grownup

Do some stretches or yoga poses

Read a book

Take a bath

Tell a silly joke

Go for a walk with your friend or grownup

Check each one when you have tried it.

Write down
your feelings

Look in the
mirror and say
something kind
to yourself

Paint or
draw

Go for
a run

Sing a
song

Take 5 deep
breaths in
and out

Listen to
music

Learn a
new fact

Dance

Talk to
your friend or
grownup

# GET SHIRTY!

Design a colorful message about positive thinking to go on the front of this t-shirt.

You can use words, logos, pictures, patterns –whatever you like!

SAY YOUR POSITIVE MESSAGE TO YOURSELF WHENEVER YOU FEEL DISCOURAGED!

Ninja Life Hacks

# TOP TIPS!

Positive Ninja loves doing things for friends and loves it when they are happy.

Doing nice things makes Positive Ninja feel good, too! Color in the shapes as you try each top tip.

Put a smiley face sticker next to your favorite tips!

Do something active every day, like jumping up and down on the spot or going for a walk.

Close your eyes and think about someone you love. Then send them positive thoughts, like "have a good day" or "be happy."

Be kind to others!

## FEELING SAD?

Talk to your grownup about it. Things feel better when you share how you feel with someone you trust.

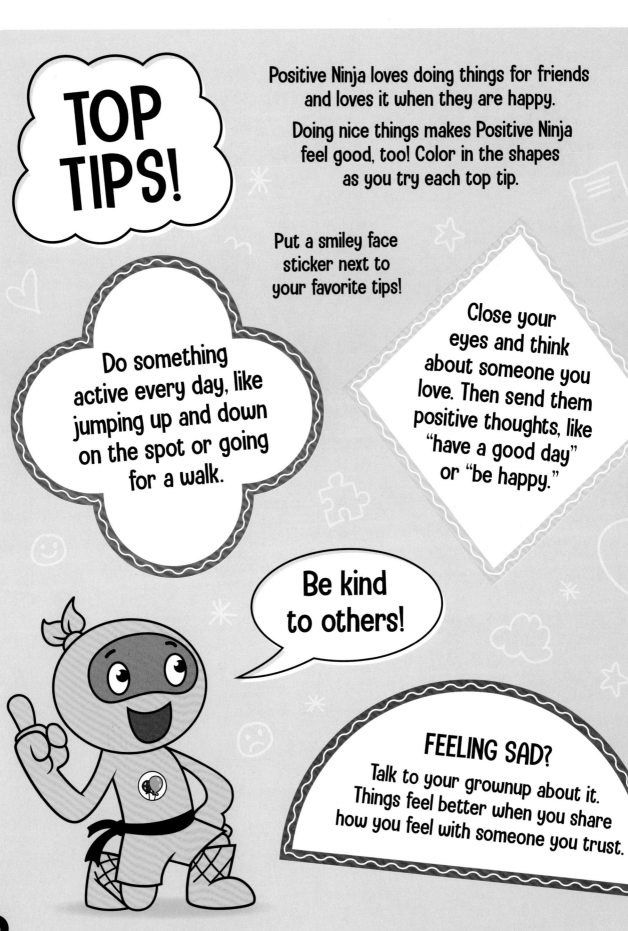

Have quiet time each day.

If you see something that makes you smile, draw a picture of it or write it down. You can look at this if you're ever having a bad day.

Close your eyes and imagine your favorite place.

Help your friend. Doing something for someone else can make you feel better, too.

Try the 1 + 3 + 10.

Say 1 calm word like "relax" or "breathe."

Then, take 3 slow, deep breaths.

Finally, count to 10.

KEEP A MEMORY JOURNAL AND FILL IT WITH MEMORIES THAT MAKE YOU SMILE!

# COLOR THE CREW

Match the letters in the color key to the pictures and color them in!

Positive Ninja

Feelings Ninja

Healthy Ninja

**COLOR KEY**

A
B
C
D
E
F

# STEP UP

Here are ways to be the best friend or sibling you can possibly be in 10 easy steps!

Color each heart a different color as you try each one.

**10** Let them borrow something of yours when they ask.

**9** Forgive them when they make a mistake. We all mess up now and then!

**8** Say sorry when you make a mistake.

**6** Listen to them.

**7** Tell them that you love them.

**4** Write them a nice note to make their day.

**5** Offer to help them with their chores.

**3** Surprise them with a random act of kindness.

**2** Make them their favorite snack.

**1** Suggest spending time together and doing something fun.

DO YOU HAVE AN IDEA OF YOUR OWN? WRITE IT HERE.
..........................................
..........................................
..........................................

How did this activity make YOU feel?

Add a thumbs up or a thumbs down sticker here.

17

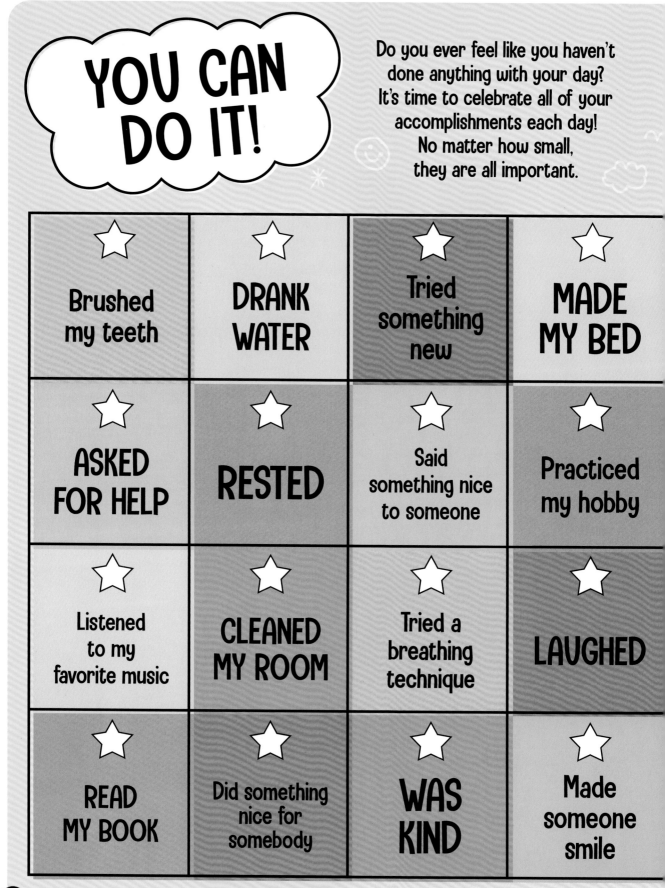

# YOU CAN DO IT!

Do you ever feel like you haven't done anything with your day? It's time to celebrate all of your accomplishments each day! No matter how small, they are all important.

| | | | |
|---|---|---|---|
| Brushed my teeth | DRANK WATER | Tried something new | MADE MY BED |
| ASKED FOR HELP | RESTED | Said something nice to someone | Practiced my hobby |
| Listened to my favorite music | CLEANED MY ROOM | Tried a breathing technique | LAUGHED |
| READ MY BOOK | Did something nice for somebody | WAS KIND | Made someone smile |

Some squares have been left blank. You can write your own ideas in these!

COLOR A STAR WHEN YOU COMPLETE EACH ACTIVITY ON THIS GRID.

| | | | |
|---|---|---|---|
| High-fived someone | HAD AN IDEA | | CALLED A FRIEND |
| WENT OUTSIDE | Made a card for someone | HELPED OUT AT HOME | Did some drawing or coloring |
| | Asked for help when I needed it | LEARNED SOMETHING NEW | Told a funny joke |
| Did something nice for myself | | How did this activity make YOU feel? Add a thumbs up or a thumbs down sticker here. | |

19

# MY VIEW

What can you see from your window?
Find somewhere comfortable to sit and
draw a picture of your view in the space.
Don't forget to color it in!

IF YOU DON'T LIKE THE VIEW FROM YOUR WINDOW, DRAW WHAT YOU WOULD LIKE TO SEE OUT THERE INSTEAD!

# WHICH NINJA ARE YOU TODAY?

Look at all of the different ninja emotions on this page and color in the one you feel like today!

It's important for us to recognize our feelings. It can help us to understand them better.

Angry Ninja

Creative Ninja

Hangry Ninja

Stressed Ninja

Disappointed Ninja

Anxious Ninja

Inventor Ninja

Listening Ninja

Zen Ninja

Impulsive Ninja

Lazy Ninja

REMEMBER, YOU CAN COLOR MORE THAN ONE.

## MAKE A WISH

Did you know that being kind to others can make YOU feel better, too?

Share some good vibes by writing down wishes for six people you care about.

**1** NAME: ..............................................

..........................................................

..........................................................

..........................................................

**2** NAME: ..............................................

..........................................................

..........................................................

..........................................................

## I hope my friend or family member . . .

. . . has a good day at school.

. . . gets a special treat.

. . . has a fun time on vacation.

. . . feels better tomorrow.

. . . gets to have ice cream for dinner.

. . . feels brave enough to try something new.

. . . gets a new pet.

You can use these ideas to help you or you can make up your own.

**WRITE THEIR NAME IN THE SPACE OR DRAW THEM—WHATEVER YOU LIKE!**

3 NAME:

4 NAME:

5 NAME:

6 NAME:

Now it's your turn. What would you wish for? Write it in the space.

# SHAPE SHIFTING

Look at all these ninjas jumping around!
Can you match up each ninja
with their shadow?
Don't forget to color them in!

How did this activity make YOU feel?

Add a thumbs up or a thumbs down sticker here.

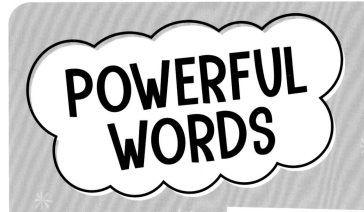

# POWERFUL WORDS

Positive Ninja has written the word "positivity" on the board. Can you think of a positive word or sentence that starts with each of the letters?

Write them in the blank spaces.

## Let's think positive...

P ...................................................................................

O ...................................................................................

S ...................................................................................

I ...................................................................................

T ...................................................................................

I ...................................................................................

V ...................................................................................

I ...................................................................................

T ...................................................................................

Y ...................................................................................

HERE'S AN EXAMPLE TO GET YOU STARTED!

I *nvite someone new to play.*

# FINISH THE FACES

Draw the different emotions on the blank ninja faces!

Why not look in a mirror to help you draw each one?

HAPPY

EXCITED

ANGRY

SURPRISED

# COLOR BY NUMBERS

Use the key to add colors to this picture of Positive Ninja floating up high.

## COLOR KEY

1
2
3
4
5
6

# PEACEFUL PLACE

Life can feel a bit busy or noisy at times, so why not imagine that you are somewhere peaceful? Finish this garden by coloring in these flowers using your favorite colors.

What beautiful blooms!

HOW DID THIS ACTIVITY MAKE YOU FEEL? CIRCLE YOUR ANSWER.

Calm     Happy     Sleepy     Something else

31

# MY WORLD

This page is a celebration of the people you love most of all! Write, check, and circle positive words to describe your friends, family, and yourself, too.

## I AM . . .

Check the positive words that describe YOU. Then write your own.

- ☐ Brave
- ☐ Happy
- ☐ Kind
- ☐ Helpful

## My FRIENDS are . . .

Check the positive words that describe your friends and then write your own.

- ☐ Fun
- ☐ Loud
- ☐ Silly
- ☐ Friendly
- ☐ Supportive

## My FRIENDS make me feel . . .

Circle the positive words that describe how your friends make you feel, and then write your own.

Safe    Loved    Confident    Happy

Ambitious

Strong

Fun

Loyal

## My FAMILY is . . .

Check the positive words that describe your family, and then write your own.

- ☐ Caring
- ☐ Unique
- ☐ Fun
- ☐ Noisy

........................................
........................................
........................................

## My FAMILY makes me feel . . .

Circle the words that describe how your family makes you feel, and then write your own in the spaces.

Safe      Calm      Happy

Smart      Warm      Loved

........................................
........................................
........................................
........................................

Generous

Helpful

Funny

How did this activity make YOU feel?

Add a thumbs up or a thumbs down sticker here.

# MAKE ME SMILE

Add a smiley face sticker next to all of the things that make you smile on this page.

WRITE OR DRAW TO FILL THIS PAGE WITH MORE THINGS THAT MAKE YOU FEEL GOOD.

# LET'S DECORATE

Doodle and color to decorate Positive Ninja's cake. You could draw stars, hearts, zigzags, dots, or whatever you like!

WHAT COLOR ICING WILL YOUR CAKE HAVE?

# LEND A HELPING HAND

Positive Ninja has lots of ideas to make other people feel good. How many of these will you try?

Check them off as you go.

HERE'S A SPACE FOR YOU TO WRITE YOUR OWN IDEAS.

- ☐ WASH or DRY THE DISHES
- ☐ SET THE TABLE
- ☐ Help to CARRY THE GROCERIES
- ☐ Join in with THE CLEANING
- ☐ MAKE A CARD for a friend or someone in your family
- ☐ HUG someone who is feeling sad
- ☐ Ask someone if they want to JOIN IN A GAME
- ☐ Help TIDY UP at home
- ☐ Ask your teacher if you can HELP THEM with a job
- ☐ Help WASH THE CAR

- ☐ ............................................
- ☐ ............................................
- ☐ ............................................
- ☐ ............................................
- ☐ ............................................
- ☐ ............................................
- ☐ ............................................

# MY HAPPY PLACE

Think of somewhere special that you love to be. It could be a place in your house, a park in your neighborhood, or somewhere you went on vacation—IT'S UP TO YOU!

Circle the words to complete these sentences.

My happy place is . . .  OUTSIDE  /  INSIDE

I go to my happy place . . .  WITH MY GROWNUP  /  BY MYSELF  /  WITH MY FAMILY

My happy place is . . .  BIG  /  SMALL

## What do YOU DO in your happy place?

Check the words that describe what you do in your happy place and then write your own.

- ☐ Draw
- ☐ Sit quietly
- ☐ Listen to music
- ☐ Close my eyes
- ☐ Think
- ☐ Walk

..............................................
..............................................
..............................................

## How do YOU FEEL in your happy place?

Check the words that describe how you feel in your happy place. You can check as many as you like!

- ☐ Happy
- ☐ Peaceful
- ☐ Calm
- ☐ Safe
- ☐ Cozy
- ☐ Warm
- ☐ Relaxed
- ☐ Sleepy

..............................................
..............................................
..............................................

SOOTHING SEA

Look at this calm picture and imagine the sound of the waves. Then use your favorite colors to finish the picture by drawing anything you like!

DOODLE SOME COLORFUL SEA CREATURES AND SHELLS.

Trace the waves with your finger.

How did this activity make YOU feel?

Add a thumbs up or a thumbs down sticker here.

# FEAST WITH FRIENDS

Sharing is always a good idea! Today each ninja has brought their favorite foods to share. What tasty treats will you spot?

THERE ARE 10 THINGS TO FIND IN THE SCENE. ADD A NINJA STICKER IN THE PANEL BELOW WHEN YOU FIND EACH ONE.

PEANUT BUTTER

# FEELING BRIGHT

Color in this ninja using your favorite colored pencils or crayons. If you can't pick just one color, then use them all and create a rainbow ninja!

CROSS OUT EVERY OTHER LETTER IN THE WHEEL TO REVEAL A POSITIVE PHRASE.

ANSWER: ___ ___ ___ ___ ___ ___ ___

WE'VE DONE THE FIRST ONE TO START YOU OFF!

GO AROUND THE WHEEL THIS WAY →

# GO OUTSIDE

Sometimes big worries can feel much smaller when you go outside. So, enjoy some open space and fresh air—there is a whole world to explore outdoors.

THE NEXT TIME YOU GO FOR A WALK WITH YOUR GROWNUP, DRAW OR WRITE ALL ABOUT IT HERE.

## I could SEE . . .

- Animals
- Trees
- Cars

## I could SMELL . . .

- Flowers
- Food
- Beach

# I could HEAR . . .

- [ ] Traffic
- [ ] Birds
- [ ] Wind

# I could TOUCH . . .

- [ ] Trees
- [ ] Grass
- [ ] Pebbles

# SIX THINGS I LOVE ABOUT ME!

Sometimes it feels easier to think of stuff you are bad at, rather than what you're good at. Write six things you love about yourself on this mirror.

## IDEAS!

I'm a good friend

I am brave

I am kind

I am smart

SAY THESE OUT LOUD TO YOURSELF EACH DAY.

1. ........................................
2. ........................................
3. ........................................
4. ........................................
5. ........................................
6. ........................................

IF YOU EVER FEEL DISCOURAGED, READ THESE TO REMIND YOU HOW GREAT YOU REALLY ARE.

# TONS OF FUN

Singing or playing music is lots of fun–and a great way to feel positive! Take a look at these musical ninjas. Can you circle the one that's not the same in each row?

**1.**

A

B

C

**2.**

A

B

C

**3.**

A

B

C

# POSITIVE VIBES

Some days it can be difficult to focus on the good things. Use this space to keep track of all the good things when they happen!

CHECK THESE OFF WHEN YOU TRY EACH ONE. USE THEM AS INSPIRATION FOR GOALS TO TRY!

## GOOD THINGS!

- ☐ I went to a party
- ☐ I made a new friend
- ☐ I tried hard at school
- ☐ I did something that scared me
- ☐ I tried a new food
- ☐ I learned a new fact
- ☐ I made something for my friend
- ☐ My friend said something nice to me
- ☐ My teacher said, "Good job!" to me
- ☐ I got to school on time
- ☐ I packed my own lunch
- ☐ I didn't give up

# POSITIVE GOALS

I visited . . . ......................................................................................................

(HOW ABOUT: friends, grandparents, a new place)

I was happy when . . . ...............................................................................

(HOW ABOUT: I did well in a spelling test, I learned a new fact, I painted a picture)

I was proud of . . . ...................................................................................

(HOW ABOUT: my brother/sister, myself, my friend)

I made myself feel better by . . . ..........................................................

(HOW ABOUT: petting my dog or cat, hugging my grownup, drawing)

I loved it when . . . ...................................................................................

(HOW ABOUT: my joke made everyone laugh, I helped someone who was having
a bad day)

How did this activity
make YOU feel?

Add a thumbs up or
a thumbs down
sticker here.

# HOW TO DRAW A NINJA

Follow this simple step-by-step and soon you will be able to draw a ninja, too!

**1** Draw a round head, like this.

**2** Add this shape in the middle of the circle for the eyes.

**3** Give your ninja eyes and a mouth. Then, draw in the knotted end of the fabric.

**4** Draw the ninja's upper body with arms crossed.

**5** Sketch the shorts and legs, and then the feet.

**6** Add some criss-cross lines to the shoes. Finally, add a belt around the waist.

PRACTICE DRAWING YOUR NINJA ON THIS PAGE BY FOLLOWING THE STEPS. WHAT COLOR WILL YOUR NINJA BE?

MY NINJA IS CALLED

## I AM GRATEFUL

Try Positive Ninja's grateful challenge with your grownup or a friend! Each day choose one idea from the list below and talk together about all the ways to be thankful. Add a butterfly sticker to each idea you discussed.

- [ ] Something that always makes you feel calm after a hard day

- [ ] A time that you tried a new food and enjoyed it

- [ ] When you volunteered for a task at school and had fun

- [ ] Your favorite teacher

- [ ] A book you read that made you feel happy

- [ ] Someone that always listens to you

- [ ] A time you listened to a friend's worries

- [ ] A favorite game that you play

- [ ] When you helped someone with a problem

IT DOESN'T MATTER WHAT ORDER YOU TRY THESE.

It's good to celebrate the things we are grateful for!

PICK ANYTHING FROM THE LIST AND DRAW OR WRITE ABOUT IT ON THIS PAGE. HOW ABOUT SKETCHING YOUR FAVORITE TEACHER, OR DESCRIBING YOUR FAVORITE BOOK OR SPORT HERE?

# SPOT THE DIFFERENCE

Spending time with friends and playing outside is the perfect way to keep a positive mindset!

Can you spot 8 differences between these two pictures of the ninjas having fun at the park?

Add a star sticker or color in the circles below for every difference you spot.

# DIG IN!

What do you love to eat?

Draw your favorite meal on this plate, then check the words that describe it.

COLOR IT IN!

**TASTE:**
- ☐ Sweet
- ☐ Spicy
- ☐ Salty

**TEXTURE:**
- ☐ Soft
- ☐ Crunchy
- ☐ Hard
- ☐ Chewy

**MAKES ME FEEL:**
- ☐ Happy
- ☐ Warm
- ☐ Full
- ☐ Cozy

# THAT'S HANDY!

Use your pencils, crayons, or markers to decorate this hand in your favorite colors and patterns. Then use it to help you breathe in and out as you trace your finger along the edge of the hand.

BREATHE IN

BREATHE OUT

YOU CAN USE THIS TECHNIQUE WHEREVER YOU GO—ALL YOU NEED ARE YOUR HANDS! IT CAN BE YOUR SECRET WEAPON FOR COPING WITH WORRY.

# A TO Z OF ME!

What positive words would you use to describe yourself? Add a word for each letter of the alphabet.

A ............................................

B ............................................

C ............................................

D ............................................

E ............................................

F ............................................

G ............................................

H ............................................

I ............................................

J ............................................

K ............................................

L ............................................

M ............................................

N ............................................

O ............................................

P ............................................

Q ............................................

R ............................................

S ............................................

T ............................................

U ............................................

V ............................................

W ............................................

e X traordinary

Y ............................................

Z ............................................

# LAUGH OUT LOUD!

Grab a pen or pencil to finish the sentences about the things that make you laugh the most. Ready, set, write . . .

Someone in my family who ALWAYS makes me laugh is ...........................................................

Someone on TV that makes me LAUGH is ...........................................................

## My FAVORITE funny TV shows!

1. ...........................................................

2. ...........................................................

3. ...........................................................

## My FAVORITE funny movies!

1. ...........................................................

2. ...........................................................

3. ...........................................................

I love making people laugh.

If something doesn't go right, sometimes it helps to see the funny side.

## My FAVORITE funny animals!

1. .................................................

2. .................................................

3. .................................................

SMILING AND LAUGHING IS GOOD FOR YOU AND CAN MAKE YOU FEEL LESS STRESSED. THE MORE YOU DO IT, THE BETTER!

## My BEST joke is:

.................................................................................

.................................................................................

.................................................................................

.................................................................................

When I have a FUNNY JOKE, I tell it to

................................................... first.

I always LAUGH when I think about

...................................................

My FUNNIEST friend is ...................................................

How did this activity make YOU feel?

Add a thumbs up or a thumbs down sticker here.

# GOODBYE GLOOM

Positive Ninja loves sunny days, but the sun is nowhere to be found. Use stickers, crayons, pencils, or markers to fill the sky with sunshine! You could also add clouds, birds, and butterflies to the scene.

A rainbow would look lovely in the sky.

# HAPPY OR SAD

All you need is a red and a blue pencil or crayon for this fun coloring challenge! Look at the pictures and color in all the things that make you happy in red, and all the things that make you sad in blue. Ready, set, go!

HAPPY

SAD

DRAW YOUR OWN HAPPY AND SAD PICTURES IN THIS SPACE AND COLOR THEM IN!

THERE'S NO RIGHT OR WRONG WITH THIS ACTIVITY—IT'S UP TO YOU TO DECIDE IF THEY MAKE YOU FEEL HAPPY OR SAD.

How did this activity make YOU feel?

Add a thumbs up or a thumbs down sticker here.

# SPOT THE DIFFERENCE

A nature walk is the perfect activity to make you feel calm and content. There's so much beauty all around you!

Can you spot 8 differences between these two pictures of the great outdoors!

Add a star sticker or color in the circles below for every difference you spot.

# MAKE A POSITIVITY JAR

Follow these simple steps to create a jar of sparkly stuff! If you're feeling sad or worried, just shake the jar and watch the swirly glitter slowly settle.

## YOU WILL NEED:

- [ ] A grownup helper
- [ ] Clear glue
- [ ] A plastic jar or bottle
- [ ] Food coloring
- [ ] Glitter

## HOW TO MAKE IT:

1. Carefully pour the clear glue into the jar or bottle until it's about one third full.

2. Next add a couple of spoons of glitter. Then add a drop or two of food coloring.

3. Fill up the rest of the bottle with warm water —make sure it's not hot!

4. Put the lid on tightly, give it a good shake, and enjoy.

How did this activity make YOU feel?

Add a thumbs up or a thumbs down sticker here.

# GROW YOUR DREAMS

Write your biggest dreams in the petals and your worst fears in the raindrops. Imagine your fears as the raindrops. They disappear into the ground and water the plant to help it bloom into a beautiful flower.

DON'T FORGET TO COLOR IN YOUR PICTURE WHEN YOU'VE FILLED IN EACH PETAL AND RAINDROP!

# MAKE IT MATCH

Can you find 5 differences between these two pictures? After you spot the differences, use your pencils or crayons to make the two pictures look exactly the same.

A

**B**

Add a balloon sticker or color in the circles below for every difference you spot.

# LET IT GO

Are your worries keeping you awake at night, or making it hard to concentrate? Positive Ninja has a smart mindfulness technique for you to try. Check it out!

## WHAT TO DO!

1. Draw or write your worries in each balloon. It could be something you're scared of, or something that makes you feel sad.

2. Close your eyes and imagine holding all of the balloons in your hands.

3. Then imagine letting them all go and watching them float up, up, and away.

4. Take a couple of deep breaths and now open your eyes.

COLOR EACH BALLOON A DIFFERENT COLOR.

How did this activity make YOU feel?

Add a thumbs up or a thumbs down sticker here.

# LOVE NATURE!

Positive Ninja is learning all about how to look after the planet with Earth Ninja. Can you find the odd one out in each row?

1.

A

B

C

2.

A

B

C

3.

A

B

C

# DOT-TO-DOT

Connect the dots to finish this picture of Positive Ninja, add the balloons emblem, then color in your creation!

# HIDE AND SEEK

The ninjas are having a party in the park. Can you find all the ninjas in the panel below in the park scene?

**Supportive Ninja**

**Sharing Ninja**

**Quiet Ninja**

**Love Ninja**

**Patient Ninja**

ADD A NINJA STICKER NEXT TO EACH NINJA WHEN YOU SPOT THEM IN THE BIG PICTURE.

Listening Ninja

Confident Ninja

Humble Ninja

Smart Ninja

Funny Ninja

# PICK ME UPS

Write down positive affirmations on pieces of paper and put them in a bag or hat. Pick an affirmation out of the bag whenever you need a little encouragement!

You are kind

You do your best

You are funny

You are loved

You try hard

You are a good friend

Saying kind things to yourself makes you feel good.

You are amazing

I love this idea!

# ALL STAR!

Fill in each star with a positive thing about YOU.

FRIENDLY

STRONG

GENTLE

# Answers:

**PAGE 13: SPECIAL DELIVERY**

**PAGE 16-17: COLOR THE CREW**

**PAGES 24-25: SHAPE SHIFTING**

**PAGE 28: ICE CREAM TIME**

**PAGE 29: COLOR BY NUMBERS**

**PAGES 40-41: FEAST WITH FRIENDS**

**PAGES 42-43: FEELING BRIGHT - "YOU CAN DO IT!"**

**PAGE 47: TONS OF FUN - 1. A, 2. C, 3. B**

**PAGES 54-55: SPOT THE DIFFERENCE**

**PAGE 66-67: SPOT THE DIFFERENCE**

**PAGE 70-71: MAKE IT MATCH**

**PAGE 74: LOVE NATURE! - 1. B, 2. C, 3. C**

**PAGE 76-77: HIDE AND SEEK**